P9-AQV-806

3- 7

Westbrook & Cleall

Reading Hymn-tunes
and
Singing Psalms

LONDON
EPWORTH PRESS

© FRANCIS B. WESTBROOK
AND CHARLES CLEALL 1969

FIRST PUBLISHED IN 1969
BY EPWORTH PRESS

Book Steward: Frank H. Cumbers

PRINTED IN GREAT BRITAIN
BY GALLIARD LTD
GREAT YARMOUTH, NORFOLK

SBN 7162 0109 7

Reading Hymn-tunes

FRANCIS B. WESTBROOK

BA, MUS D

Contents

Preface

IN 1765 Wesley published his *Grounds of Vocal Music* as an introduction to the second edition of *Hymns with Tunes Annext*. Its purpose was to enable members of the congregation to read music. It was only a brief introduction and did not cover much ground: moreover some of the directions are now obsolete. Nevertheless it did put the singer on the right track. As a bicentenary tribute, this present book has been written for the members of present-day congregations. The writer is convinced that the worshipper, even if he is not particularly musical, should have a complete edition of the hymn-book, that is, one with tunes, and should read the music as he does the words. All the difficulties he has with new tunes and even his objections to them would then automatically disappear. He believes that what Wesley aimed at in 1765 should be similarly attempted today, and in the years to come.

It is the conviction of the writer that the best way to read music is to learn it from staff notation. Once the language is firmly grasped there are no real difficulties that the beginner has to encounter. Nevertheless there are many who have some knowledge of sol-fa, and recognize the major and minor scale in sol-fa notation. For the convenience of those who know it, therefore, a brief reference is made to the sol-fa system, and one or two tunes at the beginning are set out in this notation, together with staff.

In this way the true purpose of sol-fa is preserved—to enable the singer to sing from staff through sol-fa. In the opinion of many it is a mistake to learn sol-fa and stop short at that. When the system was originated it was never intended to be separated from staff. (It may be said in passing that Wesley made no mention of sol-fa.)

It is interesting to remember that Wesley not only wrote his rudiments of music, but also included a number of exercises for the voice, 'to be got off perfectly and by heart' so that the art of singing should be thoroughly mastered. We have not ventured into this field, even though one can admire Wesley for his thoroughness. If anyone's enthusiasm raises him to this pitch, he can obtain suitable vocal exercises from any of the standard music publishers.

F. B. WESTBROOK

1. The Notes, the Clef, and the Stave

To READ a hymn-tune may at first sight seem a fearsome task: actually it is simple enough once you have grasped a few elementary principles.

Let us begin by writing out the first line of the melody, that is, the part the congregation sings, of the tune ST SAVIOUR (46 MHB). This is the language with which you will have to get familiar:

In writing music we use *notes* to express the actual tune and to tell us how long each sound should be; a stave and clef to express the pitch of the sound, high or low.

The following notes are those which are to be found in our hymn-book.

    ◦ called a semibreve or whole note
    ♩   ,,   ,, minim or half note (the one most used)
    ♩   ,,   ,, crotchet or quarter note
    ♪   ,,   ,, quaver or eighth note
    ♬   ,,   ,, semiquaver or sixteenth note

The following table will help you to remember the relative value of the notes used.

A semibreve ◦ = ♩ ♩ minims
             = ♩ ♩ ♩ ♩ crotchets
             = ♫♫ ♫♫ quavers
             = ♬♬♬♬ ♬♬♬♬ semiquavers

Another note used is called a breve ‖○‖. Two semi-breves (as the name implies) equals one breve.

In order to set down a tune, notes are placed upon a stave, which consists of five lines and four spaces:

At the beginning of the stave there is a sign known as a clef 𝄞. This clef is called the treble or G clef.

The first seven letters of the alphabet are used in naming the notes that we sing. They are placed in the stave in the following order.

E   F   G   A   B   C   D   E   F

(You can see why the G clef gets its name. It starts by being drawn through the line on which the note G stands.)

You can remember the names of the notes on the lines by the following mnemonic:

*E*very *G*ood *B*oy *D*eserves *F*avour
E   G   B   D   F

E   G   B   D   F

As for the space names, you can see that these spell the word FACE

F   A   C   E

A line written below or above the stave is called a *leger* line. The first one you will want to know is the one which marks the note C, below the line E. The line goes through the middle of the note.

C

This note is called middle C and falls roughly in the centre of the keyboard.

The note next to C, which does not have a line through it but is placed next to the line E, is D.

D

At this point it will be helpful to look at the keyboard of a piano or harmonium if you have one.

Look at the notes in the middle part of the keyboard. We will put the notes on the stave underneath. All the notes that you will be called upon to sing will be found within this compass.

A sharp or B flat		C sharp or D flat	D sharp or E flat		F sharp or G flat	G sharp or A flat	A sharp or B flat		C sharp or D flat	D sharp or E flat		F sharp or G flat	
A	B	C	D	E	F	G	A	B	C	D	E	F	G

At this stage you need not take any notice of the black notes.

Even if you cannot play the instrument you can pick out the notes with one finger.

To recapitulate:

We use various kinds of notes—semibreves, minims and so on to express musical sound and to determine how long any such sound will last.

We use a stave and a clef to determine the pitch of any given series of notes.

To name the notes we use the first seven letters of the alphabet.

2. Bars: Notes used in Hymn-tunes: Signatures: Dotted Notes: Rests

ALL TUNES are divided into bars in which there are a definite number of beats. A beat may be described as a measurement of time as long as a footstep takes to pace. The down strokes on the stave are called bar lines and the space between the lines is called a bar.

Bar

In the hymn-tunes in our book the minim is used as the standard note. There are exceptions, such as GLORY SONG (116) and OXFORD (124) where the crotchet is used: but the great majority are written in minims.

The number of minims in the bar will tell you how many beats to the bar there are. If there are two minims, there are two beats, if three, then three beats, if four, then four beats. If you look at the first bar of ST SAVIOUR (61) you will see that there are four minims to the bar. That means there are four beats to the bar. The first beat in the bar is always the strongest.

If there are more than four notes in a bar which has four beats, some of them will be of less value than a minim. There may, for example, be five notes: that means there will be two crotchets. Since two crotchets equal one minim, there will still be four minims in the bar.

If there are less than four notes in the bar which has four

beats—say three—then one of those notes will be a semi-breve. A semibreve equals two minims, so there will still be four minims to the bar.

To show the number of beats in a bar, a sign called the time-signature is used. Time signatures are not printed in tune-books these days, since it has been thought that any-one who could read music would not need to be told the time-signature of a hymn-tune. This is true, though for a beginner a time-signature would be a help. But you will encounter no difficulty if you look carefully at each bar of any given tune. You will at once be able to decide whether there are two, three or four beats to the bar. Apart from a very few exceptions all tunes have either two, three, or four beats to the bar.

A word may be added here about dotted notes. A dot by the side of a note increases its value by one half. Thus a dotted semibreve ◌· is equivalent to three minims ♩ ♩ ♩, and a dotted minim ♩· is equal to three crotchets ♪ ♪ ♪. If you look at ST SAVIOUR again you will see that there is a dotted minim for the first note in the second bar. This means that the second note, a crotchet, comes on the last half of the second beat. The final total in the bar is four beats, as in the first bar.

beats 1½ ½ 1 1

You can count as follows:

one two and three four

Little need be said about rests as you rarely see them in a hymn-tune. A semibreve rest hangs below the fourth line

6

of the bar 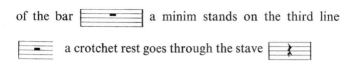 a minim stands on the third line

a crotchet rest goes through the stave

An example of a minim rest is found in RIDGE (410), where the first beat of the bar is a rest. You start singing on the second beat.

one   two

3. The Key of the Tune and the Major Scale: Sol-fa: The Sharp Keys

IT IS NOW time to consider the key in which any tune is written and the notes that are used. If you turn to ST SAVIOUR on p. 1 you will see that the line quoted starts on C.

If you play on the piano all the white notes beginning on middle C and finishing on the next C you have played the scale of C major. On the stave it will appear as follows. We will use semibreves as the notes.

C D E F G A B C

The word scale comes from the Italian *scala*, which means a ladder. That is what a scale is—a tone ladder on which you ascend or descend, step by step.

You will discover that every tune makes use of some part of the scale. Some tunes use the notes between the first and last notes of the scale only, others go outside it and use notes above and/or notes below. ST SAVIOUR uses two notes above top C.

The distance between the two Cs is called an octave. You can remember an octave as the distance between one note and the next of the same name. It can also be said to be the distance between the first and eighth note, as the word octave (from the Latin *octo* = eight) implies.

8

If you look at the diagram of the keyboard on p. 3 you will see that there are black notes between C and D and D and E, but not between E and F. Likewise there are black notes between F and G, G and A, A and B, but not between B and C.

We will now define the term *interval*. An interval is the distance between two notes, counting them, plus any that lie between. The smallest interval which can be sung or played is called a *semitone* or half-tone. There are no notes between a semitone. In the major scale there are two semitones, and these occur between the third and fourth notes and the seventh and eighth notes. In the scale of C these semitones occur between E and F and B and C.

The rest of the intervals of a scale have a note between them. The interval with a note in between is called a *tone*, and in a scale there are five in all. They lie between C and D, D and E, F and G, G and A, A and B. A major scale, therefore, consists of five tones and two semitones, the latter always occurring between the third and fourth notes and the seventh and eighth notes. When the scale is written out, the semitones are indicated by curved lines called slurs.

You may be familiar with the sol-fa system of reading music, and if you are you will recognize the major scale as doh, ray, me, fah, so, lah, te, doh. If this is a help to you, you may remember that on whatever note the major scale may start (and there are twelve in all, seven white notes, and five black) the sol-fa notation will always be the same. In the scale of C, doh is C.

Similarly, in staff notation, it can be said that whatever note the major scale starts on it will always consist of five tones and two semitones, and the two semitones will always occur between the third and fourth notes and seventh and eighth notes.

We will now write out the tune ST SAVIOUR in full. Observe that it starts on the fourth beat of the bar.

ST. SAVIOUR. Key of C; doh is C.

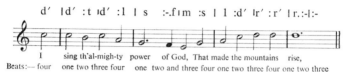

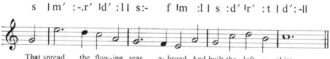

The double bar line at the end of the first line marks the end of the second line of the verse. It comes (in this instance) after the third beat of the bar. The fourth beat of that bar starts on the next line. A double bar line is also found at the end of the fourth line. All music ends with a double bar line. The last bar also has three beats to it, but as the tune starts on the fourth beat of the bar, this beat is thought of as completing the last bar. So we have in this tune eight bars, with four beats to each bar.

You will see that this tune uses all the notes in the octave except the first two.

But it uses two notes in the octave above

A good number of tunes use notes in the octave above or the octave below. Those that use notes in the former octave rarely use notes in the lower and vice versa. It would make the range too wide. A notable exception is the LONDONDERRY AIR (809). It has been suggested, not without reason, that this was originally written for the violin and not the human voice.

We may say in passing that in writing notes on the stave all notes above the third line have their tails pointing downwards: all those below it, upwards. On the third line itself tails can point either upwards or downwards. When there are two lines of melody on the same stave, as you will see in the tune book, the upper part has all the tails upwards and the lower part all the tails downwards.

As an exercise play and sing through ST SAVIOUR.

To repeat, a major scale can start on any one of the twelve notes between the two Cs and it will always sound the same, no matter on what note it starts. It always consists of five tones and two semitones, and the two semitones always occur between the third and fourth notes and seventh and eighth notes.

The next scale in order after C starts on G, five notes above, or four notes below. In sol-fa notation doh is G.

Written down, the scale of G looks like this

Scale of G.

If you look closely you will see that the first four notes

are the same as the last four notes of the scale of C. The scale of G, therefore, follows on from the scale of C.

In the last four notes you will observe a difference in the seventh note. This has a sharp to it, and the note, one of the black notes, is called F sharp. The sharp sign is indicated as follows, ♯, and it raises a note by a semitone, in this case from F to F sharp. The sharp sign is always placed at the beginning of the line, immediately after the clef and is known as the key signature. The key signature of one sharp means that the scale (or tune) is in the key of G major.

The reason that there is an F sharp in the key of G is to keep the last semitone between the seventh and eighth notes. If there was no F sharp the semitone would fall between E and F, the sixth and seventh notes, and we thus would not get a major scale.

Let us look at a tune in the key of G major, all the notes of which will be found in the scale of G major. We will choose NORTH COATES (286).

NORTH COATES   Key of G

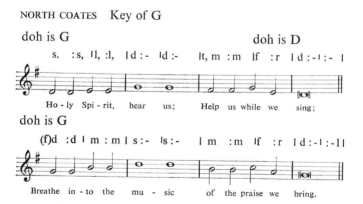

This tune begins below the G on the stave, but the notes are all in the key: they belong to the octave that starts on the G below middle C.

The key signature, though written on the top line, affects all the Fs on the stave. Thus the F on the first space is a sharp as well.

As in ST SAVIOUR, the double bar line at the end of the first line marks the end of the second line of the verse, but unlike ST SAVIOUR it coincides with the end of the ordinary bar. Sometimes this double bar line occurs at the end of the third line of the verse as in TRUST AND OBEY (516). Remember that a double bar line always comes at the conclusion of a tune, wherever else it may occur.

You can see there are four beats to the bar in this tune as with ST SAVIOUR. But NORTH COATES begins on the first beat of the bar.

As an exercise, play and sing through the tune.

The next scale following on after G is D. To get the notes on the stave we will start four notes below the G on the stave. As was the case in the previous scale, the first four notes of the scale of D form the last four notes of the scale of G.

In order to keep the semitone between the seventh and eighth notes we must put a sharp in front of the seventh note C, which raises it to C sharp. Thus the scale will have two sharps.

For a tune in the key of D let us turn to STRACATHRO (102 MHB).

This tune has three beats to the bar, and starts on the last beat of the bar.

One or two points call for mention. The tune has some slurs. Slurs are always put over notes where they are sung to more than one syllable or word. (Note, for example, the slur in the third bar, which covers the two notes sung for the first syllable of the word 'ever'.)

If we count in *strict* time there are only two beats given to the semibreve at the end of the second line of the verse on the word 'free'. In certain tunes, however, and STRACATHRO is one of them, it is customary, though not necessary, for the note to be lengthened at this point for five beats.

As the tune is written, there are only two beats given to the last note. The third beat is regarded as having come at the beginning of the tune, which starts on the third beat. As in the case of the second line, however, it is usual for the last note to be prolonged a little.

For an exercise, pick out the tune on the piano and sing it.

The next scale in order will be A. The pattern will be the same as in the previous ones. The last four notes of the scale of D will form the first four notes of the scale of A, and the seventh note, G, will be sharpened. The scale of A, therefore, has three sharps.

Scale of A

The hymn-tunes we sing in this key will not as a general rule go beyond E. Notes in the octave below are often used, as in the key of G. This is the case in the tune SPANISH CHANT (769) which we will take as an example. There are two beats to the bar.

SPANISH CHANT   Key of A: doh is A

Bread of heaven, on Thee I feed, For Thy flesh is

meat in - deed: Ev - er may my soul be fed

With this true and liv - ing bread; Day by day with

strength sup - plied Through the life of Him who died.

As an exercise play and sing through SPANISH CHANT. You should by this time come to recognize not only the keys of the tunes but the intervals between the notes. You will *see* as well as hear the difference in the sound of notes that are two, three, and four notes (and so on) away from each other.

Our final scale—in sharps—will be E. There are others:
but as the tune-book has no tune which contains more than
four sharps we need not consider them.

The first four notes of the scale of E are the same as the
last four notes of the scale of A. The seventh note is raised
by a semitone to D sharp.

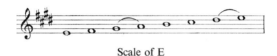

Scale of E

As an example of a tune in the key of E we can look at
MARYTON (32). You will see that there are three beats to the
bar. It overflows into the octave below in the last bar but
one, where we have a C sharp and D sharp below the E.

MARYTON   Key of E

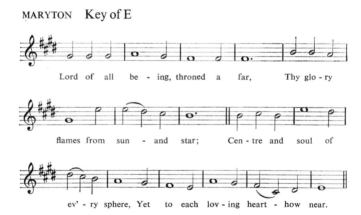

Lord of all   be - ing, throned   a   far,   Thy glo - ry

flames from   sun - and   star;   Cen - tre and   soul   of

ev' - ry sphere, Yet   to   each lov - ing heart - how   near.

As an exercise play and sing through MARYTON.

4. The Flat Keys

HAVING dealt with the tunes that are written in scales with sharps we will now turn to those written in flats. The sign of a flat is ♭ and it lowers a note by a semitone, just as a sharp raises a note by a semitone. A major scale in a flat key is constructed in exactly the same way as a major scale in a sharp key. There are five tones and two semitones, the latter falling between the third and fourth notes and the seventh and eighth notes.

If you look at the diagram on p. 3 you will see that the black notes are called both sharps and flats. When the key is a flat key the black note is called a flat, e.g. E flat. When in a sharp key the same note will be called D sharp.

The scale that has one flat is F and the note that is flattened is B. When we make a new sharp key we always raise the seventh note by a semitone. When we make a new flat key we always flatten the fourth note by a semitone.

To find the scale of F we move backwards five notes, or forward four notes from C. To get the scale on the stave in its entirety we will move forward four notes.

Scale of F

For a tune in the key of F let us take ST FLAVIAN (43)

You will see that ST FLAVIAN has four beats to the bar and starts on the fourth beat of the bar.

As an exercise play and sing through the tune. (Don't forget that the B in bar three is B flat.)

The next flat scale in order is **B flat**. This is the first time
we have had a scale starting on a black note. We move back
five notes from F to get our starting point: and the next
note to flatten is E flat, to get the semitone between the third
and fourth notes.

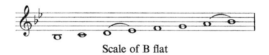

Scale of B flat

As an example of a tune in the scale we will take NATIVITY
(85).

NATIVITY   Key of B flat

You will note that there are four beats to the bar. There
are two crotchets for the second beat in the first bar, and
there is a dotted minim on the third beat of the second bar.

18

The final note of the bar, a crotchet, comes in on the last half beat of the bar.

Play and sing the tune through.

This remark applies to all succeeding tunes.

The next flat scale is E flat.

Moving back five notes (or forward four notes) from B flat we flatten the A to get the semitone between the third and fourth notes. We will move forward four notes to place the scale on the stave.

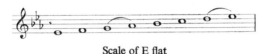

Scale of E flat

For an example of a tune in this scale let us take KILMARNOCK (50).

KILMARNOCK   Key of E flat

The Lord's my Shep-herd, I'll not want; He makes me down to __ lie In pas-tures green; He lead-eth me The qui - et__ wa - ters by.

This tune has four beats to the bar and starts on the fourth beat. Note that some beats have two notes (crotchets) to them.

Finally we come to the scale of A flat. We move down five notes from E flat and flatten the D.

Scale of A flat

For a tune written in this scale we will choose ST BEES (432).

ST BEES   Key of A flat

Hark my soul! it is the Lord; 'Tis thy Sa-viour, hear His word:

Je-sus speaks, and speaks to thee: Say, poor sin-ner, lov'st thou Me?

Note that this is in four pulse measure. Some of the notes go into the octave above. This is quite common with tunes in A flat. HANOVER (8) for example is written between the E flat of the octave of the scale as we have written it and the E flat of the scale above. The same can be said for the great majority of tunes in the key of F, G, A and B flat. They are found roughly between the fifth note of the lower octave and the fifth note of the upper.

The next scale in order is D flat. The note to be flattened is G. There are, however, only three tunes in this key in the book: REST (825), PRAISE (487), and SLEEPERS WAKE (255), and these are not often sung. So we will not write the scale out. For those who are interested we will complete the number of major scales in use in the Appendix. In the key of D flat it will be G that is flattened.

5. Tunes in the Minor Keys: the Sharp Keys

IT IS NOW time to turn to the tunes in what are known as the minor keys. These are written in the minor scale.

Turn to the chart on p. 3 and play the scale of C major.

This is called C major because the interval between C and E is a major third, consisting of two tones.*

The scale of C minor has this difference. In playing it up the keyboard you put your finger on the black note of E flat, not E. The interval between C and E flat is a minor third, consisting of a tone and a semitone. Hence the scale is called C minor.

Here it is written out

Scale of C minor, ascending

One or two points call for comment. The semitones occur between the second and third notes and the seventh and eighth notes. The key signature of the minor scale is always that which starts on the third of the scale, in this case E flat. This is because the key of E flat is known as the relative major key. The relative minor key of any major key is always found a minor third below. Thus the relative minor of the key of E flat major is C minor. The relative minor of the key of C major will accordingly be A minor. What is called the tonic minor key of a major key, however, starts

* A tone is a major second, and a semitone a minor second.

21

on the same note. Thus the tonic minor of C major is C minor, and the tonic minor of E flat major is E flat minor. The same principle holds good for all keys.

It cannot be denied, in spite of the foregoing explanation, that the key signature of the minor scale is a clumsy one. In the scale of C minor we have to put in a natural ♮ by A and another by B in order to write the scale correctly. (The natural sign ♮ raises a flat by a semitone, and lowers a sharp by a semitone.) Unsatisfactory as the system is, however, we cannot change it now. Actually, the E flat signature suits the scale quite well as it descends, because B and A are changed into B flat and A flat. Remember, then, that the key-signature of a minor scale is always that of the relative major scale, which starts on a note a minor third above the note on which the minor scale starts.

Scale of C minor, descending

Observe that in the descending form of the scale the semitones occur between the fifth and sixth notes and the second and third notes.

The foregoing form of the minor scale is called the melodic minor. There is another, called the harmonic minor, but as this is not used in writing hymn-tunes we will not consider it here. Those who are interested can find a note on it in the Appendix.

In the sol-fa system, the first note of the scale is not doh but lah. The ascending form of the scale runs as follows:

lah te doh ray me fe se lah. (fe is sometimes called bai.)

Descending it will be:

lah soh fah me ray doh te lah.

In treating tunes in the minor scale we will start with A minor. That is because there are no sharps or flats in the key signature, the relative major scale being C. But in the ascending form, the sixth note will be F sharp and the seventh note G sharp.

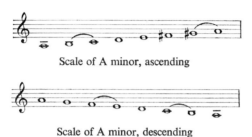

Scale of A minor, ascending

Scale of A minor, descending

For a tune in A minor let us turn to LEICESTER (500), a beautiful one written by John Bishop (1665–1737).

LEICESTER   Key of A minor

Peace, doubt ing heart! my God's I__ am: Who formed me man, for -bids my fear; The Lord hath called me by my name: The Lord pro-tects, for __ ev - -er near; His blood for me did once a - tone, And still He __ loves and guards His own.

Observe that the tune has four beats to the bar, beginning on the fourth beat. In the second bar, the tune

23

goes into the octave above the one in which we wrote the scale. You have seen this procedure before. Note the natural (♮) in the third bar. Normally a sharp or a flat only lasts for a bar, so that the natural sign is really superfluous. It is, however, put in as a precautionary measure, in case a singer should sing a G sharp instead of a G natural, as it comes very close to the G sharp in the second bar.

The next scale in order is five notes on from A to E minor. In order to keep the semitone between the second and third notes we must raise the second one, F, by a semitone, making it F sharp. The sixth and seventh notes will be sharps, but these are not shown in the key signature.

Scale of E minor, ascending

Scale of E minor, descending

For a tune in E minor we will choose SOUTHWELL (239). SOUTHWELL   Key of E minor: lah is E

SOUTHWELL is simple and straightforward, with four beats to the bar, beginning on the fourth beat.

B minor is the next scale five notes on from E, or four notes back. We will write it out in the octave beginning on B below middle C. C will be the note to be sharpened, and, as before, the sixth and seventh notes will have sharps not shown in the key signature.

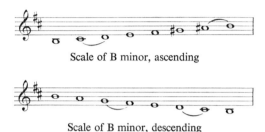

Scale of B minor, ascending

Scale of B minor, descending

There are hardly any tunes in B minor in the hymn-book. One, LANSDOWN (371) begins in B minor, but the last line moves into the relative major, and so finishes in D major.

LANSDOWN   Key of B minor. lah is B

And can it be that I should gain An in‑t'rest in the Sa‑viour's blood?

Died He for me, who caused His pain? For me, who Him to death pur‑sued?

A‑maz‑ing love! how can it be That Thou, my God, shouldst die for me!

This tune has three beats to the bar. Observe the note in the last bar but one in the second line—the E sharp on the syllable 'pur-' of 'pursued'. This sharp raises the E a semitone. On the piano or organ this is the same note as F.

The next scale is F sharp minor—five notes on from B. The note to be raised a semitone is G.

Scale of F sharp minor, ascending

Scale of F sharp minor, descending

There is only one tune in the book in F sharp minor—WARWICK GARDENS (98) by T. C. Gregory.

This fine tune is not often sung, partly because it is difficult to learn. Once it is known, however, it is invariably liked. We will set it out here.

WARWICK GARDENS   Key of F sharp minor: lah is F sharp

Note that the tune has four beats to the bar, beginning on the fourth beat.

The B sharp in the third and fourth bars of the second line is the same note as C on the piano. This B sharp is due to the fact that the tune here moves into the key of C sharp minor, the next in order to F sharp minor.

26

6. Tunes in the Minor Keys: the Flat Keys

STARTING from A minor and moving back five notes, or forward four notes we come to D minor. The key signature is B flat, the same as for the scale of F major, and it is B that is flattened throughout. This is six notes from the key note D. Observe, however, that in the ascending form of the scale the B flat is turned into a B natural.

Scale of D minor, ascending

Scale of D minor, descending

For a tune in D minor let us look at Dykes's well-known ST CROSS (187).

ST CROSS   Key of D minor

O come and mourn with me a - while;   O come ye to the Sa-viour's side

O come, to- geth-er let us mourn: Je - sus, our Lord, is cru - ci - fied

The tune has four beats to the bar. Remember that a breve is equal to two semibreves and four minims. Notice the interesting variant at the beginning of the second line, where the tune starts on the fourth beat of the bar.

The next scale in order is G minor. Moving back five notes from D or four notes forward we come to G. The note to be flattened is E. The key signature is the same as that for B flat major, but the E has a natural for the ascending form of the scale.

Scale of G minor, ascending

Scale of G minor, descending

A good example of a tune in G minor is ST BRIDE (81).

ST BRIDE   Key of G minor

This tune has four beats to the bar and begins on the fourth beat. It moves into the octave below in the first, third, and sixth bars.

The next scale in order is C minor, moving back five notes from G or four notes onward we come to C. The note to be flattened is A. The key signature is the same as that for E flat major.

Scale of C minor, ascending

Scale of C minor, descending

For a tune in C minor we cannot choose a better than MEINE HOFFNUNG (My hope) (70).

MEINE HOFFNUNG   Key of C minor

This tune has four beats in the bar. Note that in the last bar but one the first four notes of the ascending scale occur. This tune goes into the octave above in the first, second, fifth, sixth, and ninth bars.

Finally we come to the scale of F minor. We move four notes on or five notes back from C. The note to be flattened is D. The key signature is the same as for A flat major.

Scale of F minor, ascending

Scale of F minor, descending

There are only a few tunes in F minor in the book. A lesser known, but expressive one, UFFINGHAM (570) by Jeremiah Clark will serve as a good example.

UFFINGHAM Key of F minor

Ho-ly,__ and true, and right-eous Lord, I wait to prove Thy perfect will;

Be mindful of Thy gra - cious word, And stamp me with Thy Spi - rit's seal.

This tune has three beats to the bar. In the first and second bars the tune moves into the octave below. Note that in the fourth and fourteenth bars the E natural in the octave below also occurs. We have seen before how some tunes move in two octaves.

You should now be able to read any tune that you find in the hymn-book. If you want to know whether the tune is in a major or a minor key, look at the last note. If the key is major, the tune will always (or almost always) finish on the key note. If the key is minor, it will finish on the note a minor third below the key note of the key signature.

Thus if the key signature is one sharp and the last note is E then clearly the key is E minor. If the last note is G then it will be G major. There are some exceptions to this. Thus in the case of the PASSION CHORALE (202) and LANSDOWN (371) the tunes start in the minor key and finish in the relative major. The PASSION CHORALE has E as the last note in the melody; but the last bass note is C, showing that the tune finishes in the key of C major. A similar case is that of MORECAMBE (688). The tune is in C major, but the last note of the melody is G. Here again, however, the last bass note is C. The bass note invariably ends on the key note, whether the tune is major or minor.

If you make a practice of singing or playing through at least one tune a day it will not be long before you can read any tune quite easily.

7. The Bass Clef

FOR THOSE who can read from a bass clef, a simple introduction such as this is scarcely necessary, because you will have already learned to read your notes. For those, however, who wish to know something about it and have learned nothing previously, the following explanation is given.

Let us look at the keyboard once more. This time we will start from F.

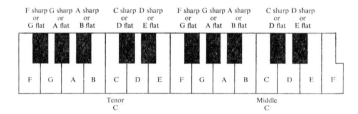

Find middle C on the piano: on the above diagram it is the one nearest the right hand of the page. The C eight notes below is called tenor C. It gets its name from the fact that tenor voice starts from this note. Its range is from this C to the G or A above middle C.

The F above tenor C is the note on which the bass clef (or F clef as it is sometimes called) is placed.

F

32

The two dots marked on either side of the fourth line, in front of the clef mark out the line as F.

Thus the notes are put in different places in this clef from those in the treble clef. The notes nevertheless follow on in alphabetical order as in the G clef.

F G A B C D E F G A B C

Notes above middle C are to be found: for these leger lines are used.

D E F G

As you will know the bass clef is used for those who sing the bass and tenor portions of a hymn-tune. As an example we will take WINCHESTER OLD (129).

This is in the key of F major and has four beats to the bar, beginning on the fourth beat.

WINCHESTER OLD   Key of F

While shep-herds watched their flocks by night, All seat-ed on the ground,

The an - gel of the Lord came down, And glo - ry shone a - round.

As an exercise pick this out on the keyboard with two fingers!

33

8. Compound Time

IT IS NECESSARY to add a chapter on this subject because some of the simplest tunes in the book are written in compound time. All the tunes we have hitherto considered have been written in simple time—that is, where the unit of measurement has been a single note, usually a minim. When there are two, three, or four *dotted* notes to the bar the time is compound.

We will take as an example TRUSTING JESUS (517). This tune has two dotted crotchets to a bar, though for the most part the bars are made up of a crotchet and a quaver, followed by another crotchet and a quaver. You will remember that a dot increases the value of a note by one half, so the quaver represents the dot of the crotchet. In this tune a dotted crotchet occurs at the end of every second bar, representing the second beat.

We will write out the tune of the verse. The chorus is constructed on the same principle.

TRUSTING JESUS

In BLESSED ASSURANCE (422) we have an example of compound time where there are three beats to the bar, represented by three dotted minims. We will give the first line of the tune. It begins on the last beat of the bar.

BLESSED ASSURANCE

CHRIST RECEIVETH (322) is an interesting example. The verse is in simple time, with three crotchet beats to the bar, starting on the last beat of the bar. The chorus is in compound time, with four dotted crotchets to the bar, starting on the last beat of the bar.

Other examples of compound time are WOODFORD GREEN (119) and ORIENT (132) with two dotted crotchets to the bar and IN DULCI JUBILO (143) with two dotted minims to the bar.

9. Tunes in Free Rhythm

A FEW TUNES have no bars to them at all. These tunes
are in free rhythm, i.e. there is no definite beat to be given
to them. They were written in the old days before strict
time was introduced. A good example is ADORO TE (691
second tune). It is not difficult to read. Each bar line marks
off the end of a line. Where there is a slur, you sing one
word or syllable to the notes contained within it. The point
about these old melodies is that you sing the words as you
would say them. Thus they represent a good halfway house
to the practice of chanting the psalms.

Here is the first line of 691:

ADORO TE

Sa - viour a - gain ___ to Thy dear name we raise

The pause mark at the end ⌢ means that you stay a little
while on the note.

VEXILLA REGIS (184) looks a little more formidable.
Actually it is not really difficult. The same principle has to
be borne in mind. There are no definite beats to the bar.
The words are sung as they would be spoken. The lines
binding the minims (called ligatures) look strange. Actually
they represent slurs. It would have been better if this tune
has been written out with slurs, like ADORO TE. Here is the
first line:

The roy — al ban — — ners for — — ward go;

Just a word about the key signature. This tune is not in a major or minor scale, but in one of the modes—the scales that were in existence before our major and minor ones were established. It is in the Dorian or first mode. This normally starts on D and consists of all the white notes between the two Ds. Here it is transposed to start on F and so some flats must be added to get the intervals in the right place.

First or Dorian mode (transposed to F)

Sometimes—as here—the sixth note was flattened through-out the melody. D flats therefore are inserted when necessary. The first mode, however, normally has D natural (or B natural when it starts on D) for the sixth note.

The other two VENI CREATOR (779) and ANNUE CHRISTE (641) are comparatively simple. VENI CREATOR is written in the seventh mode (or Mixo-Lydian). It starts on G and consists of all the white notes between the octave. Here it is transposed down a tone to start on F. So flats have to be introduced to keep the semitones in the right place. They occur between the third and fourth and sixth and seventh notes.

You will see that the tune finishes on the note F. ANNUE CHRISTE is a fairly modern tune, written in the style of an old tune. The composer has written it in the key of G major. We do not often sing the hymn, but the melody is a very fine one.

NEARER MY GOD TO THEE (468 third tune) is a modern tune in free rhythm. It starts in D minor and then, passing through many modulations, finishes on a chord in D major. In the last verse the final chord is in A major.

In addition to the tunes written in free rhythm there are some tunes which have irregular barring, thus approaching the style of those written in free rhythm. A notable example is LOVE UNKNOWN (144) where some bars consist of three minims and others of two minims. Three bars which have three beats to them are the first, ninth, tenth, and last. (The last beat of the last bar occurs at the beginning of the tune.) Another example is OLD 124th (912) where the last bar but one has three semibreves. The rest have two semibreves to the bar. The fourth bar of MYLON (831) has four beats to the bar while the rest (except the last) have three.

You should now have sufficient knowledge to read any tune in the hymn-book. If you give as much time as you can to practice you will discover that in a year or so you will have gained all the facility you need to sing at sight. You will, moreover, never want to be without your tune-book, and you will realize how much you missed in using a book of words only. Thus your knowledge of the simple rudiments of music will enable you to fulfil the injunction of the apostle St Paul to sing praises with understanding.

Appendix

EACH TUNE is headed by a metre. The most frequent metres are S.M., C.M., and L.M.—verses of four lines each. S.M., as its letters imply, stands for short metre.

In a short metre verse there are six syllables in the first, second, and fourth lines and eight in the third. Accordingly there will be six notes to each of the first, second, and fourth lines and eight notes to the third. Where there are more notes than these, some are slurred so as to be sung to one syllable. See for example the first bar in the second line of ST GILES (708). The second beat has two notes to it but they are crotchets, equalling one minim and sung to the word 'our' in the first verse.

C.M. stands for common metre, which has eight syllables for the first and third lines, and six syllables for the second and fourth. (See RICHMOND or LYDIA (1)). L.M. stands for long metre which has eight syllables for all four lines.

If you look at the metrical index at the end of the tune book you will see each tune classified according to its metre. The figures in each case refer to the number of syllables in each line of the verse.

One or two more points call for explanation. Where there are two consecutive figures without a full stop in between it means that those two lines are rhymed. See for example REVERENCE (537). Here the metre is marked 88.88.4.

> 'Tis not to ask for gifts alone, }
> I kneel in prayer before His throne; }
> But, seeking fellowship divine, }
> I feel His love, and know it mine, }
>   When I can pray.

Where two consecutive lines are not rhymed a full stop always occurs—e.g. ST CUTHBERT (283) 8.6.8.4.

> Our blest Redeemer, ere He breathed
> His tender last farewell,
> A Guide, a Comforter bequeathed,
> With us to dwell.

Here the first and third lines rhyme and the second and fourth.

Some 8.7.8.7. tunes are called Iambic. An Iamb is a metrical foot of two syllables which go from weak to strong. An example is DOMINUS REGIT ME (76).

The Kĭng ŏf lóve mў shépherd ĭs.

Those which are not so called are in Trochaic measure.

A Trochee is a metrical foot with two syllables which go from strong to weak. See CROSS OF JESUS (318)

Sóuls ŏf mén whў wíll yĕ scátter ...

Some 10.10.10.10. verses are called Dactylic. A Dactyl is a metrical foot of three syllables—long, short, short. See GLORY SONG (116).

Sing we the King who is coming to reign, ...

The ordinary 10.10.10.10.s usually go in Iambic measures—

Abide with me, fast falls the eventide,—

though the tune obscures this outline, in the way in which it flows.

Further information on metre can be gained by studying a book such as *The Elocutionist's Cyclopaedic Handbook* by C. Egerton Lowe.

INTERVALS

A WORD may be added about the intervals that are found in the tunes which we sing. You will remember that we defined an interval as the distance between two notes, counting them, plus any that lie between (see p. 9). We have already learned that a semitone is the smallest interval that can be sung, since there are no notes in between. A semitone is called a minor second, and a tone a major second, consisting of two semitones. Note that intervals may either ascend or descend. Here they are given in the ascending form. Those set out below are all to be found in the keys of either C major or C minor.

minor second   major second
(semitone)   (tone)

The other intervals which you will sing are a minor third, consisting of a tone and a semitone:

minor third

a major third, consisting of two tones:

major third

a perfect fourth, consisting of two tones and a semitone:

perfect fourth

a perfect fifth, consisting of two tones, a semitone and a tone:

perfect fifth

a minor sixth, consisting of two tones, a semitone, a tone, and a semitone:

minor sixth

a major sixth, consisting of two tones, a semitone and two tones:

major sixth

a minor seventh, consisting of two tones, a semitone, two tones and semitone:

minor seventh

This, however, usually starts on a different degree of the scale from that of the first. In GOPSAL (247) it starts on the eighth and drops to the second.

minor seventh

In RICHMOND (1) in the Key of G major, it starts on the fifth note and drops to the sixth in the octave below.

minor seventh

The interval of the minor seventh sometimes starts on the fifth note. The fifth note of the scale is called the dominant, and the seventh above it is the dominant seventh. You get an example in ASCENSION (410) which is in the key of F major. Hence the fifth note is C and the seventh above is B flat.

dominant seventh

The octave is also used:

octave

Also what is called the diminished fifth, consisting of a semitone, two tones and a semitone:

diminished fifth

An example can be seen in BENEATH THE CROSS OF JESUS (197) last bar but one:

diminished fifth. Key, E flat major

Also NICHT SO TRAURIG, which means 'Not so sad' (189), first and second bars:

diminished fifth. Key, G minor

A very rare one (in hymn-tunes) is the diminished fourth, consisting of a semitone, tone, semitone. See DAVID'S HARP (340) sixth bar.

diminished fourth

Key, D major: but the tune at this point has moved into B minor

It should be added that the number of tones and semitones in any given interval always remains the same, no matter on what degree of the scale they start, even though the order may be different. For example, D to G is a perfect fourth:

perfect fourth

and consists of two tones and a semitone. But the order in this case is tone, semitone, tone. (D to E, E to F, F to G.)

In ST SAVIOUR (p10) the first tune we studied, there is a minor third (C to A) in the first bar, another (E to G) in the second bar; a major sixth (G to E) at the beginning of the second line, and a perfect fourth (E to A) in the sixth bar. Remember that an interval can either ascend or descend.

You should now experience no difficulty in recognizing any interval in the tunes of the book, no matter what the key.

The last sharp key we learned was that of E (see p. 16). The next in order will be B with 5 sharps.

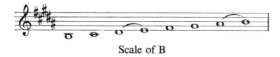

Scale of B

You can start to write the scale either on the B below middle C or on the B on the third line of the stave.

The next is F sharp.

Scale of F sharp

The sharp added for the seventh note E sharp will be F on the piano. In the scale of F sharp, however, this will be called E sharp. The eighth note, like the first, will be F sharp.

Finally C sharp.

Scale of C sharp

Here every note in the scale of C is sharpened. The seventh note, B sharp, will be C on the piano: but it is always called B sharp in the scale of C sharp.

There is very little music written in this last key; and not a great deal in the two former. As was said in Chapter IV there are no tunes in the Methodist Hymn Book in any of these keys.

The last flat key we dealt with was A flat (see p. 19). Three others remain. The first is D flat with five flats, referred to on p. 20. On the piano the scale of D flat will sound the same as C sharp.

The second is G flat with six flats. On the piano it will sound the same as F sharp.

The third is C flat, where every note is flattened. On the piano it will sound the same as the scale of B.

You will sometimes see music written in the scale of G flat, but hardly any in C flat. The relative minors—E flat minor and A flat minor—are occasionally used.

HARMONIC MINOR SCALE

The minor scale spoken of in Chapter VI is known as the *melodic* minor scale. There is another called the harmonic minor scale which is represented as follows.

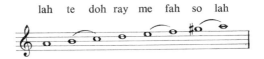

You will note

1. There are *three* semitones, between the second and third notes, the fifth and sixth notes, and seventh and eighth notes.

2. There is rather a big jump between the sixth and seventh note, consisting of a tone and a semitone. It is called an augmented second.

3. The harmonic minor scale is the same descending as ascending.

It gets its name 'harmonic', because from it are derived the harmonies used in music written in a minor key. The melodic minor scale, on the other hand, is chiefly used for a melody in the minor key. When we are thinking of the melody of a hymn-tune, therefore, it is the melodic minor form that has to be considered, though the melodic form of the scale *can* be used in harmony. The harmonic minor scale is never used as a melody, with that awkward interval between the sixth and seventh notes. (There may be exceptions to this: but the average singer of hymn-tunes has no need to concern himself with them!)

If your appetite has been whetted to inquire further into the fascinating study of *The Rudiments of Music*, you should get either Stewart Macpherson's or William Lovelock's book with that title.

Index

Tunes Referred to

ADORO TE

ANNUE CHRISTE

ASCENSION

BENEATH THE CROSS

BLESSED ASSURANCE

CHRIST RECEIVETH

CROSS OF JESUS

DOMINUS REGIT ME

GLORY SONG

GOPSAL

HANOVER

IN DULCI JUBILO

KILMARNOCK

LANSDOWN

LEICESTER

LOVE UNKNOWN

LYDIA

MARYTON

MEINE HOFFNUNG

MORECAMBE

MYLON

NATIVITY

NEARER MY GOD
  TO THEE

NICHT SO TRAURIG

NORTH COATES

ORIENT

OXFORD

PASSION CHORALE

PRAISE

REST

REVERENCE

RICHMOND

ST BEES

ST BRIDE

ST CROSS

ST CUTHBERT

ST FLAVIAN

ST GILES

ST SAVIOUR

SLEEPERS WAKE

SPANISH CHANT

STRACATHRO

TRUSTING JESUS

UFFINGHAM

VENI CREATOR

VEXILLA REGIS

WARWICK GARDENS

WINCHESTER OLD

WOODFORD GREEN

Authentic Chanting

CHARLES CLEALL

MA, B MUS, ADCM

Commissioned by The Royal School of Church Music
The Selection and Training of Mixed Choirs in Churches
(1960, Independent Press Ltd)

John Merbecke's Music for the Congregation at Holy Communion
(1963, Epworth Press)

Commissioned by The Tyndale Fellowship for Biblical Research
Music and Holiness (1964, Epworth Press)

Sixty Songs from Sankey
(1966, revised edition, Marshall, Morgan, & Scott Ltd)

Plainsong for Pleasure
Hymns to Span the Christian Year
(1969, Gospel Music Publishers)

Commissioned by The London Association of Organists
Voice Production in Choral Technique
(1969, revised edition incorporating 'Scientific Aspects of Sound,
Speech and Song'; and 'The Natural Pitch of the Human Voice';
Novello & Co Ltd)

AUTHENTIC CHANTING (1)

Two Principles

IS THERE a rarer musical virtue?

Explicably rare, perhaps; for 'good chanting of the psalms is the greatest difficulty which has to be faced by even a cathedral choir, which sings the psalms every day.'[1]

Yet 'the singing of the psalms and the reading of the lessons are the two basic elements' of the Daily Offices; in spite of an 'increasing and deplorable tendency to lose sight of this responsibility.

'Too often, the clergyman seems to take the minimum now provided as an encouragement to fall below it, and to think that one psalm is sufficient. It cannot be too strongly asserted that this practice robs Divine Service of a large part of its inspiration.'[2]

'Not only our people, but some of our clergymen, are slowly losing any spiritual knowledge of the Psalter as a whole. That spiritual knowledge has, in every age, been the main sustainer of the soul of man apart from sacraments and prayer; and the main vehicle of the praise of God even *in* the sacraments.

'The Psalter . . . brings to the worshipper's heart and lips the perfect devotional life of Jesus, Who lived and died by it. Furthermore, it joins him to the vast company in Heaven and on earth who, day by day, week by week, month by month, year by year, have striven to form their lives on Jesu's life; and to praise the Father as He did in His holy Manhood on earth.

'Do we clergymen choose a single psalm (almost invariably the shortest available) for each of our public

Offices? Do we permit it to be carelessly and hastily read, instead of reverently sung, where that is feasible? Do we thus suggest that the Psalter is an encumbrance, to be perfunctorily dealt with, till we gain sufficient iconoclastic courage to abandon it, and substitute a gospel hymn?

'If so, we strike at the very life of all sound church music, because we cut off the main stream of Christian praise.'[3]

It may be that we should chant the psalms better if we knew more of their structure and tradition of performance.

Of their structure, in that, 'as literature, they are unique: they are poetry which is not dependent on rhythm or metre. The first half of each verse presents a thought to the mind: the second half contains another thought which is either the antithesis or the complement of the first';[4] for which reason, 'their chief formal characteristic, the most obvious element of pattern, is fortunately one that survives in translation.'[5]

Of their tradition of performance, because that tradition came into being to serve and convey the meaning of the words. Its chief feature is 'a pause which is called the Caesura'—'after the Mediation, or cadence *in the middle of the verse*'—'which is most important. Its purpose is two-fold: (i) to allow time for breath; (ii) to bring out the form of the Hebrew poetry. This pause is an integral part of the rhythm.'[6]

Indeed, 'the pause at the colon is all-important',[7] and 'must be jealously guarded', because 'there is a tendency for it to disappear.'[8]

Without the Caesura, chanting makes us breathless and fatigued (especially if we are old), and leaves us no time to take in the meaning of the words.

Where the Caesura is not evident, it is safe to say that the structure and tradition of performance of the psalms is inadequately known and understood. That tradition is set out in the following pages; which are claimed, not in the least to be original, but to reflect authentically the mind of

2

the Church, as expressed by her leading writers and scholars.

The main principle is that of the Gregorian Tones

First, it is necessary to assert that 'the commonly supposed clear distinction between plainchant and Anglican chant is, in principle, non-existent.' We cannot say, 'Ah, but you only do that in plainsong,' because 'Anglican chant is an off-shoot of the harmonized plainchant which was common throughout Christendom during the sixteenth and seventeenth centuries. The principle of the Gregorian and the Anglican is the same.'[9]

Secondly, we cannot brush away the tradition of the Caesura, for example, on the ground that it is to be observed only when the psalms are said; for 'the nearer the chanting approaches good reading, the better it is. An Anglican chant is, after all, merely a vehicle for sacred and poetic words.'[10] 'Saying the psalms is not so very different from singing them.'[7]

'Have we not rather misled people by speaking of *singing* the psalms? If we remember that chanting is merely reading with inflexions, we shall have a much clearer idea as to the method of performance. . . . The more we regard the process as organized and inflected reading, the nearer we shall approach an ideal performance.'[11]

With this in mind, we see why tradition bids us, 'Recite the whole *mezza-voce*, rather than sing it':[12] 'The voice must not be used at its full power.'[13]

Of course, *good* reading is no mean achievement: 'it is little less difficult to get a congregation to *say* the psalms decently than to *sing* them decently.'[14]

All the syllables have equal time-value

We cannot validly distinguish between plainchant to Latin words and Anglican chant to English words.

'In English, the accented syllable snatches up and hurries

3

on the other syllables'; and, 'in Latin, the unaccented syllables are allowed to take their own time';[15] yet, in both, 'the basic principle is that all the notes have equal time-value.'[16]

Does that seem revolutionary?

Yet 'the manner in which chanting takes the rhythm of the words is precisely the manner in which the words deliver their rhythm: that is, by enunciating certain syllables with a stronger emphasis than others . . . but it is an emphasis of stress; or weight; or pressing: not of lengthening the time-value.

'Carefully yet naturally enunciated, all the syllables have *practically* an equal time-value; and it is just that degree of equality which is intended when we speak of all notes in chanting as having an equal time-value.

'In the course of natural speech, it is obvious that the word "strength" will take a slightly longer time to pronounce than the word "with"; but, if the natural enunciation is good, the time-relationship of the two words will certainly be nearer a pair of quavers than a dotted quaver and a semiquaver.'[17] (See footnote *).

* The reader must know that no less distinguished an authority than Don Anselm Hughes, o.s.b., calls it a 'false premiss that all notes are essentially equal in length', and says that, 'while plainsong sung in notes of equal time-value is possible in Latin (though, we maintain, not historically or theoretically lawful), it is quite impossible in English' (*Plainsong for English Choirs*, 1966, Faith Press, pp. 68 f.). It looks as though Don Anselm contradicts us; but he is talking, not of chanting, but of plainsong in the sense of a body of times with specific note-values including the *bistropha* and *tristropha*, which manifest accent by prolonging duration. Don Anselm himself says that 'there is no sort of accent which does not involve some tiny degree of prolongation; but these nuances are not deliberate extensions in time, and they should in no case be allowed to deteriorate into a double-note (for which purpose the chant provides a *bistropha*') (p. 40). Now we have but to think through Dr J. H. Arnold's words (reference 17) in conjunction with this last sentence by Don Anselm to see that syllables of unit-length is not only a *possible* principle in English, but the foundation of all authentic chanting—and of all eloquent speech, as our best actors demonstrate.

'It is unfortunately true that many choirs . . . have mistaken "speech rhythm" as meaning that the psalms should be sung at the pace of normal speech; whereas in fact the chanting of "speech rhythm" must be considerably slower and broader than ordinary conversation.'[18] 'For the rhythm of the recitation and inflexions alike, one is best guided by solemn speech; in which all syllables tend to become more equally spaced than in conversation, and unaccented syllables to be given their just value.'[19]

It is, above all, 'equality of syllables which gives great resonance and beauty to the text.'[20]

We shall now pursue these principles further; both to understand them better, and to take account of their exceptions.

REFERENCES

[1] *Music in Church*, the Report of the Archbishops' Committee (Church Information Office, 1948; revised edition, 1960), p. 33.

[2] Ibid, p. 15.

[3] *Church Music in History and Practice*, by the Revd Winfred Douglas (1935; revised edition, Faber, 1963), p. 114.

[4] *A Grammar of Plainsong*, by a Benedictine of Stanbrook (Rushworth & Dreaper, 1934), p. 61.

[5] *Reflections on the Psalms*, by C. S. Lewis (1958; Fontana Books, 1961), p. 11.

[6] *A Grammar of Plainsong*, p. 63.

[7] *Music in Church*, p. 16.

[8] *Plainsong Accompaniment*, by J. H. Arnold (1927; Waltham Forest Books Ltd, second edition, 1964), p. 101.

[9] *The Oxford Companion to Music* (ninth edition, 1955), pp. 32, 33.

[10] Ibid, p. 35.

[11] *The Complete Organist*, by Harvey Grace (The Richards Press, 1920), p. 189.

[12] *A Manual of Plainsong*, by Briggs & Frere (1902; revised edition, Novello & Co Ltd, 1951), p. viii.

[13] *A Grammar of Plainsong*, p. 58.

[14] *The Background of the Prayer Book*, by C. S. Phillips (SPCK, 1938), p. 138.

[15] *A Grammar of Plainsong,* p. 17.
[16] *Plainsong Accompaniment*, p. 5.
[17] Ibid, p. 11.
[18] *Music in Church*, p. 36.
[19] *A Manual of Plainsong*, p. ix.
[20] *A Grammar of Plainsong*, p. 17.

AUTHENTIC CHANTING (2)

Eight Rules

1. *'Do not hurry the syllables sung on the reciting-note, or drag those which fall to the inflexion.'*[12] Remember that 'the tendency of choirs and congregations is to gabble the recitation, and dawdle over the rest of the music; and this has to be guarded against.'[10]

'If the speed of the words taken to the reciting-note be slightly retarded, and the speed of the words taken to the cadence slightly hastened, an evenness of speed will result; and one of the great objections to Anglican chanting will be removed.'[21]

'Singers are asked, not so much to create a suitable rhythm, as to avoid destroying a rhythm which is already there.'[22] 'The words have a rhythm of their own; rather more regular than that which would be produced if they were read in a speaking voice, but quite distinct from the duple or triple time of modern measured music. When the psalms are chanted, the music must therefore follow this rhythm, so that both recitation and inflexion will be in the same tempo.'[23]

'The smallest rhythmic figure is the foot, which . . . may contain two or three beats *of equal length*. A foot of two beats is called a duple foot; one of three beats, a triple foot.'[24]

In the examples which follow, the tune is William Croft's chant in A minor, No. 103 in *The Anglican Chant Book*; and the words are taken from *The Revised Psalter Pointed*, Psalm 38.

Ex. 1

3. There is no health in my flesh be-cause of Thy dis-pleas-ure:

2. 'If the recitation is taken too quickly, there will be an unconscious effort to complete the rhythm by a pause before the inflexion; but, if it be deliberate and rhythmical, it will flow easily into the inflexion, the rhythm of which will be of the same character as that of the recitation. In other words, *the inflexion must begin without the slightest gap immediately after the last note of the recitation.*'[23]

Ex. 2

1. Put me not to re-buke O Lord in Thine ang - er:

3. 'If the reciting-note has only one or two syllables assigned to it, the reciting-chord should not be held longer than is necessary for the clear pronunciation of the syllable or syllables in question';[21] so that *the recitation may be but a quaver in length.*

Ex. 3(a)   Ex. 3(b)

5b. By reas-on of my fool-ish-n'ss.*   22. Haste Thee to help me:

* Note shading of vowel.

4. In theory, 'there should be no break whatever between verse and verse, or verse and *Gloria*';[8] in practice, 'there need be no more interval between the verses than is necessary to make the alternation of voices clear, and to prevent the drowning of the sostenuto on the last note of one verse by the beginning of the next':[25] which means, in effect, that '*the pause between the verses . . . equals one crotchet*',[26] or duple foot.

Ex. 4

5. 'The psalmody should be so animated as to allow each half-verse to be sung in one breath. If the first half of a verse be too long to admit of this, it is subdivided by a pause called the Flex.* Taking the quaver as the average length of notes, we make the note immediately before the Flex a crotchet. At this place, a breath may be taken; but the pause must not be so long as to interrupt the flow of the psalmody.'[27]

As we have seen, 'no break between verses' means, in effect, a pause of one duple foot. In the same way, *the Flex means a note (or, if the preceding note is verbally or musically stronger, two notes each) of one duple foot, followed by a rest of the same length.*

---

* So named because, in plainsong, 'immediately before this pause, the melody falls by one diatonic interval, unless this is a semitone, in which case the fall is a minor third'.[6] For our purpose, its secondary meaning of a breathing space other than the Mediation or final Cadence is what matters.

9

Ex. 5

13. But as for me,   I am like a deaf man and hear, not:

6. 'Psalters which have a fondness for two or more syllables on the final chord of the cadence (sometimes called a "postman's knock") need not be abandoned. This inartistic effect can quite well be cured by the deliberate smoothing out and evening up of the final syllables.'[21]

We can assign a definite meaning to 'smoothing out and evening up'; as we can to 'rallentando' in rule 7. The fact is, *wherever we 'need to take a breath', the last note 'becomes doubled in length'*; or, *if it be the second of a duple foot* (see rule 7, paragraph four), *'both notes become doubled, and the last one softened.'*[19]

Ex. 6

Gloria: As it was in the be-gin-ning,   is now and ev-er shall   be:

* This rest becomes a quaver to accommodate the upbeat syllable following, so that 'now' shall fall on the first beat of a duple foot.

7. 'A definite pause should be made at the colon; long enough to cause an observable cessation of vocal sound in the building whatever its size.'[25]

'In singing the psalms, this pause at the colon should be *especially marked*: it is a great aid to proper chanting. . . . Many people forget that the title-page of the Prayer Book draws attention to the great importance of this colon point, both for singing and for saying.'[28]

'The pause of silence at the colon marking the half-verse (long enough, it has been suggested, mentally to repeat the words "Deep breath")' is of 'two outstanding characteristics' by which anyone who has heard 'a competent choir ... cannot fail to have been most forcibly impressed.'[29]

The other is 'the combined diminuendo and rallentando immediately before the colon and similarly at the end of the verse',[29] and at the Flex; 'confined to the two notes' ending the phrase concerned; 'or to the last note alone, if the penultimate note (either for verbal or musical reasons) is not the stronger of the two'.

The difference between the Caesura and the other two pauses (Flex and Cadence) is that, accepting the suggestion that we mentally repeat the words 'Deep breath', if we articulate the p of 'Deep', *the Caesura is a break of* TWO *duple feet*; whereas the Flex and the Cadence make a break of *one* duple foot.

'All choirs have not the same tradition in this respect; but, however briskly the psalms may be sung, and whatever may be the tendency to shorten the pauses, a certain ratio should be observed. *The pause at the Mediation is to be longer than the pause between the verses.*'[26]

Ex. 7

17. Tru-ly I am read-y to fall: and my pain is ev-er with me.

8. 'The singers' part' at the Caesura 'is silence; but a combined silencing of voices and organ may be rather too abrupt to be pleasant';[8] in which case, *the organist may*

(*i*) '*tide over the pause by transferring the last chord of the Mediation to the Swell with his left hand,* as soon as the voices have attacked the last note, *holding it there till the second half is reopened on the Great*:'[8]

Ex. 8(a)   Organ accompaniment to Ex. 7

or (*ii*) '*the whole chord may simply be held over*':[8]

Ex. 8(b)   Alternative Organ accompaniment to Ex. 7

REFERENCES

[6] *A Grammar of Plainsong,* p. 63

[8] *Plainsong Accompaniment,* by J. H. Arnold (1927; Waltham Forest Books Ltd, second edition, 1964), p. 101.

[10] *The Oxford Companion to Music* (ninth edition, 1955), p. 35.

[12] *A Manual of Plainsong,* by Briggs & Frere (1902; revised edition, Novello & Co Ltd, 1951), p. viii.

[19] Ibid, p. ix

[21] *The Organization and Training of Parish Choirs,* by Francis T. Kennard (The proprietors of *Musical Opinion,* 1925), p. 64.

22 *A Grammar of Plainsong*, p. 43.
23 *A Manual of Plainsong*, p. xiv.
24 *A Grammar of Plainsong*, p. 46.
25 *A Manual of Plainsong*, p. xiii-xiv.
26 *A Grammar of Plainsong*, p. 69.
27 Ibid, p. 68.
28 *The Parson's Handbook*, by the Revd Percy Dearmer (OUP, twelfth edition, 1932; eighth impression, 1962), p. 186.
29 *Plainsong Accompaniment*, p. 94.

SUMMARY FOR CHOIRS

The Secret of Good Chanting

1. *'All the syllables have* practically *an equal time-value.* It is obvious that the word "strength" will take a slightly longer time to pronounce than the word "with"; but, if the natural enunciation is good, the time-relationship will certainly be nearer a pair of quavers than a dotted quaver and a semiquaver.'[1] It is, above all, 'equality of syllables which gives great resonance and beauty to the text'.[2]

2. *Wherever we 'need to take breath', the last note 'becomes doubled in length'* (or, if the previous note is verbally or musically the stronger, *'both notes become doubled, and the last one softened'*).[3]

3. *The 'pause between the verses',* or between verse and *Gloria,* or for breath other than at the colon, *'equals one crotchet'.*[4]

4. 'A definite pause should be made at the colon';[5] in fact, *'the pause at the colon is all-important',*[6] *and 'should be especially marked'.*[7] It should be 'long enough mentally to repeat the words "Deep breath" '.[8] 'The pause at the colon is to be longer than the pause between the verses.'[4]

5. 'If the reciting-note has only one or two syllables assigned to it, the reciting-chord should not be held longer than is necessary for the clear pronunciation of the syllable or syllables in question.'[9] *The recitation may be only one quaver in length.*

6. *'The chanting of speech-rhythm must be considerably slower and broader than ordinary conversation.'*[10] 'One is best guided by solemn speech, in which all syllables tend to

14

become more equally spaced than in conversation, and unaccented syllables to be given their just value.'[3]

REFERENCES

[1] *Plainsong Accompaniment,* by J. H. Arnold (Waltham Forest Books Ltd, second edition, 1964), p. 11.

[2] *A Grammar of Plainsong,* by a Benedictine of Stanbrook (Rushworth & Dreaper Ltd, 1934), p. 17.

[3] *A Manual of Plainsong,* by Briggs & Frere (Novello & Co Ltd, revised edition, 1951), p. ix.

[4] *A Grammar of Plainsong,* p. 69.

[5] *A Manual of Plainsong,* p. xiii.

[6] *Music in Church,* the Report of the Archbishops' Committee (Church Information Office, revised edition, 1964), p. 16.

[7] *The Parson's Handbook,* by the Revd Percy Dearmer (Oxford, twelfth edition, eighth impression, 1962), p. 186.

[8] *Plainsong Accompaniment,* p. 94.

[9] *The Organisation and Training of Parish Choirs,* by Francis T. Kennard (The proprietors of *Musical Opinion,* 1925), p. 64.

[10] *Music in Church,* p. 36.

N.B. 'The commonly supposed clear distinction between plain chant and Anglican chant is, in principle, non-existent. The principle of the Gregorian and the Anglican is the same' (*The Oxford Companion to Music,* ninth edition, 1955, pp. 32, 33).

3·202